THE SECRETS OF TREES

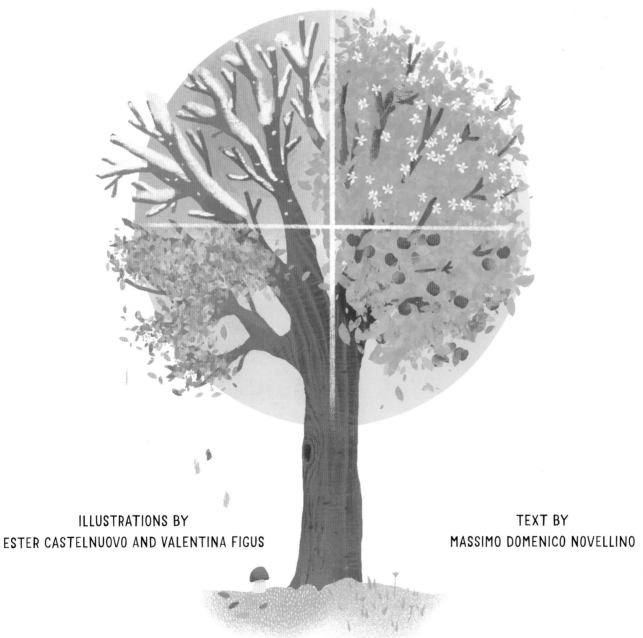

ILLUSTRATIONS BY
ESTER CASTELNUOVO AND VALENTINA FIGUS

TEXT BY
MASSIMO DOMENICO NOVELLINO

whitestar·kids

CONTENTS

HOW OFTEN DO THE TREES ALL AROUND US, RIGHT IN FRONT OF OUR EYES, GO COMPLETELY UNNOTICED?

We're so used to being surrounded by these silent, unmoving friends that we sometimes forget that they're living beings just like us: they're "born," they fight to grow, and they eat, breathe, and communicate. Plus, they're even able to move and forge solid friendships that can be quite surprising!

THANKS TO THIS BOOK, YOU'LL DISCOVER THAT THE LIVES OF TREES ARE MORE COMPLICATED THAN YOU MIGHT HAVE THOUGHT AND THAT THEY AREN'T SO DIFFERENT FROM OURS!

Browse the pages
that follow in search
of FUN FACTS and
INCREDIBLE WORLD RECORDS.
When you come across especially complex
scientific terms, don't worry!
Just look for the GLOSSARY
at the bottom of the page.

THE EVOLUTION OF PLANTS

The history of plants begins **billions of years ago**: like many other organisms, plants first appeared in the **sea**, in the form of algae made up of a single cell.

They then evolved into **the vast, diverse species** that we find today in every habitat on our planet.

TAKE A LOOK AT THE TIMELINE SHOWN HERE, GOING FROM LEFT TO RIGHT, TO DISCOVER SOME OF THE MOST IMPORTANT STEPS IN THE HISTORY OF PLANT EVOLUTION.

GREEN ALGAE

Green algae are the **ancestors** of the plants that populate our planet, still present in different aquatic settings (lakes, rivers, lagoons, seas, etc.), where they can live as **single cells** or in **colonies**.

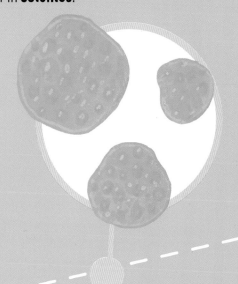

MOSS

Some of the first plants to grow **outside of water**, moss species today can be found in the coolest, most shaded zones of different habitats. To reproduce, they use tiny **spores** that are blown about by the wind.

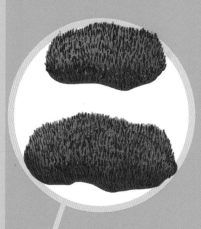

PTERIDOPHYTES

They were the first plants to grow **roots, trunks, and leaves**. They reproduce via spores, which are often gathered in small "buttons" on the underside of their leaves. They include **ferns**, Lycopodium, and Equisetum. There are fewer of them and they're less developed than in the past, when they could grow to be **many feet high**, acting as nourishment for lots of animals, including **dinosaurs**!

1500   500   420

MILLIONS OF YEARS AGO

SEED PLANTS

FLOWERING PLANTS

GYMNOSPERMS

They're the first plants to have developed **seeds**, a fundamental revolution because, thanks to those seeds, these plants could make do without water for their reproduction, necessary to moss and ferns.

Today, gymnosperms include plants such as **conifers** (pines, firs, larches, etc.) and some small shrubs.

DICOTYLEDONS AND MONOCOTYLEDONS

Dicotyledons and monocotyledons are part of a category of plants called **angiosperms**, also known as **flowering plants**. Compared to gymnosperms, they produce **flowers** to attract **insects** and **fruit** to hold their seeds. Flower and fruit serve to be more successful in reproduction as they can be dispersed more effectively.

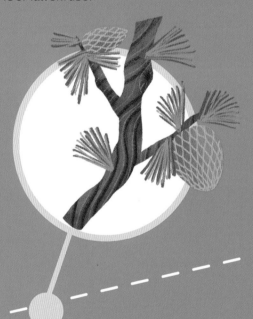

300

150

MILLIONS OF YEARS AGO

BIOMES OF THE WORLD

A **BIOME** is a vast part of the world characterized by dominating plants and a certain climate that, interacting with each other, create a distinct, unique, and balanced community.

STUDY THE MAP TO DISCOVER THE WORLD'S BIOMES AND THE MOST COMMON TREES WITHIN THEM.

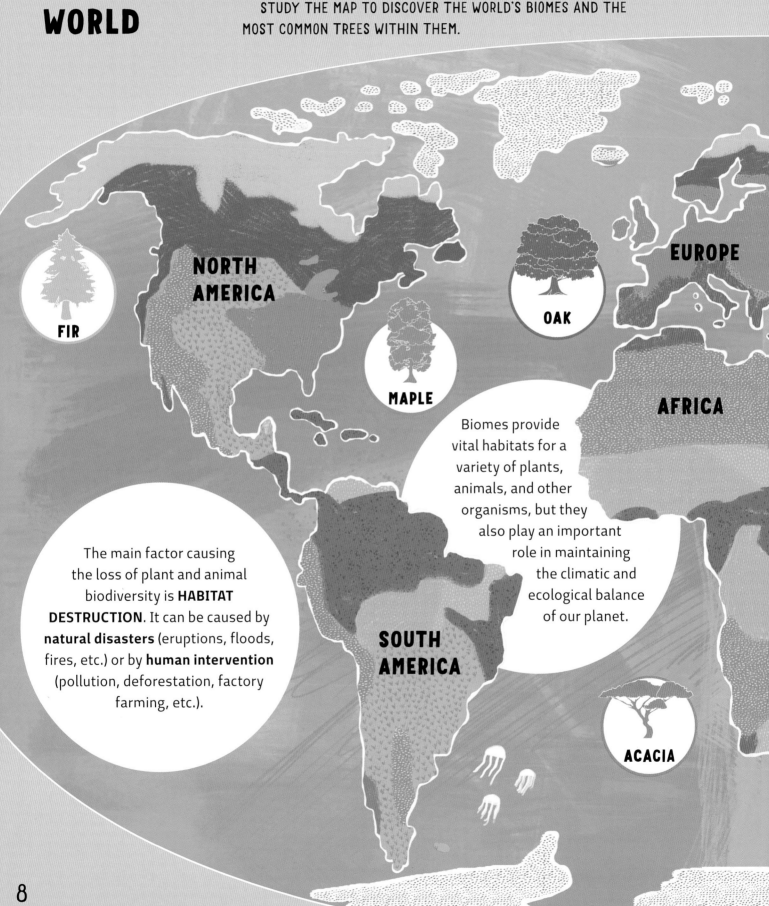

FIR

NORTH AMERICA

MAPLE

OAK

EUROPE

AFRICA

Biomes provide vital habitats for a variety of plants, animals, and other organisms, but they also play an important role in maintaining the climatic and ecological balance of our planet.

The main factor causing the loss of plant and animal biodiversity is **HABITAT DESTRUCTION**. It can be caused by **natural disasters** (eruptions, floods, fires, etc.) or by **human intervention** (pollution, deforestation, factory farming, etc.).

SOUTH AMERICA

ACACIA

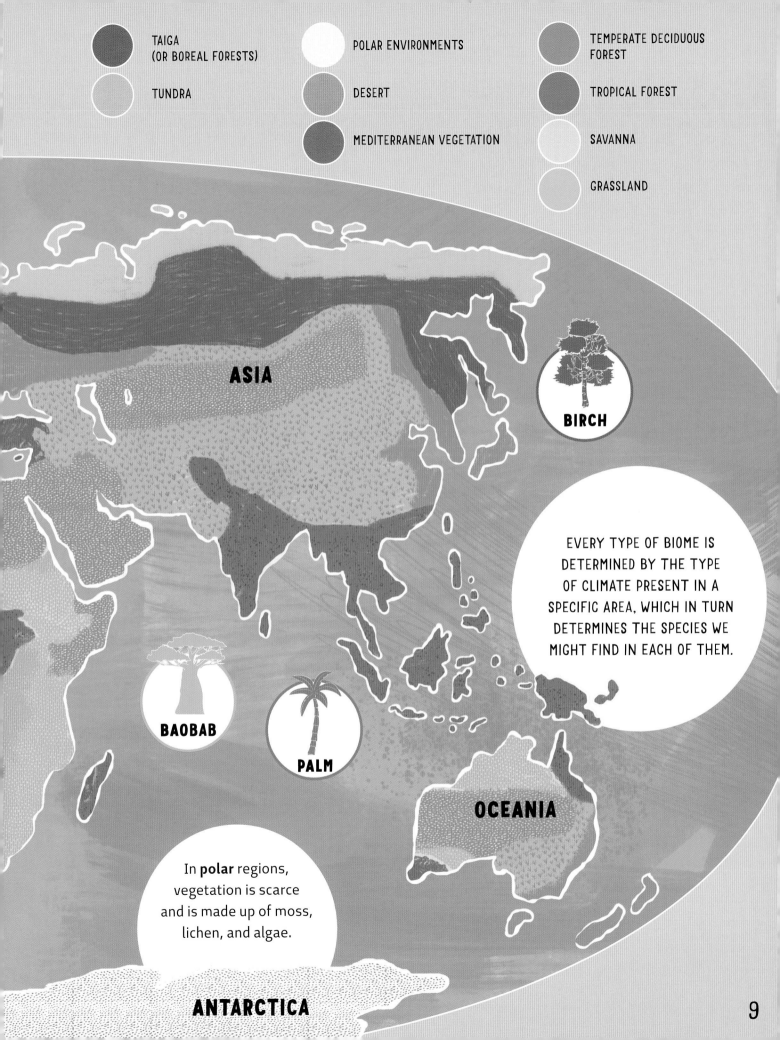

TAIGA (OR BOREAL FORESTS)

TUNDRA

POLAR ENVIRONMENTS

DESERT

MEDITERRANEAN VEGETATION

TEMPERATE DECIDUOUS FOREST

TROPICAL FOREST

SAVANNA

GRASSLAND

ASIA

BIRCH

BAOBAB

PALM

EVERY TYPE OF BIOME IS DETERMINED BY THE TYPE OF CLIMATE PRESENT IN A SPECIFIC AREA, WHICH IN TURN DETERMINES THE SPECIES WE MIGHT FIND IN EACH OF THEM.

OCEANIA

In **polar** regions, vegetation is scarce and is made up of moss, lichen, and algae.

ANTARCTICA

WHICH BIOME IS HOME TO TREES?

Trees don't grow in all biomes. They're practically non-existent in the tundra, for example, and the vegetation there is mainly moss and lichen.

 ANNUAL RAINFALL

MAXIMUM AND MINIMUM TEMPERATURE

LET'S TAKE A CLOSER LOOK AT THE AREAS IN WHICH TREES CAN LIVE AND DISCOVER THE CHARACTERISTICS OF THESE BIOMES.

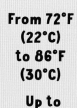

From 72°F (22°C) to 86°F (30°C)

Up to 394 in (10,000 mm)!

▪ TROPICAL FORESTS

In the areas covered by tropical forests, the climate is warm and very rainy. The plants and trees here, which have not just light but also lots of water available all year round, grow quickly, giving rise to expansive forests rich in biodiversity.

▪ MEDITERRANEAN VEGETATION

Also called Mediterranean maquis, this sort of vegetation is found all around the Mediterranean basin, but as you can see on the map, it's also found in other parts of the planet.

Warm and dry in summer and temperate in fall and winter, the climate facilitates the growth of vegetation constituted of trees and shrubs with hard leaves that can stand up to high temperatures.

From 41°F (5°C) to 104°F (40°C)

From 12 in (300 mm) to 39 in (1,000 mm)

▪ THE TAIGA (OR BOREAL FORESTS)

Cold temperatures and snow are the stars of this biome most of the year. Despite these harsh conditions, you might still find large, expansive forests of conifers such as firs (classic Christmas trees!) and pines, but also birch trees.

From -58°F (-50°C) to 50°F (10°C)

From 6 in (150 mm) to 24 in (600 mm)

▪ TEMPERATE DECIDUOUS FORESTS

This biome, which is found in areas with a temperate climate, is characterized by expansive forests of deciduous trees (which lose their leaves in winter), such as beech, maple, oak, and linden trees, in which the seasonal cycle can thus be fully observed.

From -4°F (-20°C) to 95°F (35°C)

From 20 in (500 mm) to 47 in (1,200 mm)

IF YOU WANT TO KNOW WHAT THE SEASONAL CYCLE IS, GO TO PAGE 28.

From 73°F (23°C) to 99°F (37°C)

From 39 in (1,000 mm) to 59 in (1,500 mm)

▪ SAVANNAS

Savannas are characterized by a dry season, without rain, and a wet season, during which it rains a lot. The most common trees are baobabs and acacias.

CHAPTER 1

TREE SHAPES AND PARTS

Tree "bodies" include different organs, just like our bodies.

There are three main organs in any tree:

CROWN

TRUNK

ROOTS

Their shape and purpose vary greatly depending on the species, with characteristics that can sometimes be very strange!

TREE SHAPES

Even if no two trees are exactly alike, each type of foliage can be generalized into a few outlines and shapes, which can be made out from far away.

THESE ARE THE MAIN SHAPES OF TREE FOLIAGE AND CROWNS, BASED ON THE CHARACTERISTICS OF THEIR BRANCHES AND LEAVES.

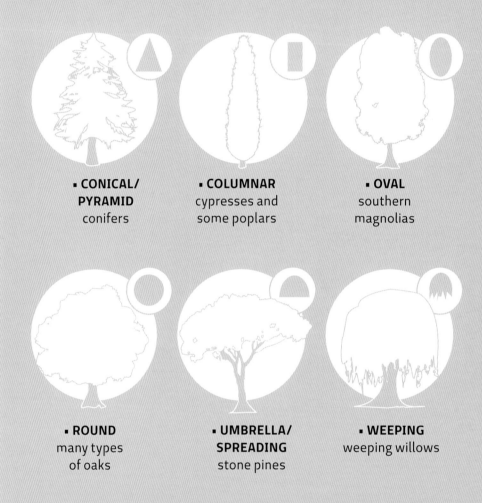

- **CONICAL/ PYRAMID**
conifers

- **COLUMNAR**
cypresses and some poplars

- **OVAL**
southern magnolias

- **ROUND**
many types of oaks

- **UMBRELLA/ SPREADING**
stone pines

- **WEEPING**
weeping willows

TO SURVIVE IN DIFFERENT CLIMATES, TREES HAVE LEARNED TO CHANGE THEIR SHAPE ACCORDING TO THE ENVIRONMENT.

In **colder** regions, for example, we often find trees that can stand up to freezing temperatures, but also those that shed their leaves before heading into long winters.

AND HOW HAVE TREES IN DRY REGIONS ADAPTED? KEEP READING TO LEARN ALL ABOUT THIS AND OTHER EXAMPLES OF ADAPTATION!

INCREDIBLE ADAPTATION STRATEGIES

BAOBABS AND OTHER BOTTLE TREES

These trees are found in **dry environments**, and their trunk has transformed into a giant cylinder able to **collect and store water**. That makes it possible for baobab trees to survive, even during hot, dry African summers.

LIKE A GIANT BOTTLE!

CYPRESS TREES AND OTHER SPECIES THAT LIVE IN WINDY AREAS

The trunks of these trees are made of a type of wood that's very **durable**, yet also flexible. The trunk, branches, and leaves grow and bend depending on the way the wind blows.

LIKE OUR HAIR WHEN WE BLOW-DRY IT!

TWISTED TREES

Sometimes, during a tree's lifetime, the surrounding environment changes. Imagine if you were stuck in one place forever: what could you do, for example, if a boulder fell next to you?
You could grow around it!

When outside factors limit a tree's ability to grow vertically, it will be forced to twist as it grows. But, as soon as it gets the chance, it will start to grow vertically again.

THESE SPECIMENS RECOUNT THE STORY OF THEIR ENVIRONMENT!

RECORD-SETTING TREES!

Within the varied world of trees, there is a lot of **diversity**, and every species has adopted the best strategies possible in order to **survive**. Evolution has led to such drastic changes so as to achieve **world records** in the plant world!

THE WORLD'S LARGEST TREE

THE WORLD'S TALLEST TREE

Giant sequoia
These trees are the **biggest and heaviest on the planet**. They live in California, where they make up immense forests.

Sequoia sempervirens
The tallest known living tree in the world is called Hyperion. It's a coast redwood (*Sequoia sempervirens*) in California.

Some sequoias are over 360 ft (110 m) tall...

...TALLER THAN A 30-STORY BUILDING!

Dwarf willow

THE WORLD'S SMALLEST TREE

This tree is truly tiny! A few leaves grow on its trunk, which reaches a height of **just a few inches**. Dwarf willows (*Salix herbacea*) live near mountains, where they make up expansive **micro-forests**!

Bristlecone pine

The world's oldest tree is over 5,000 years old!
Even the leaves on this species are long-lived:
it seems they can last up to 40 years!

IN SOME WAY, TIME DOESN'T GO BY FOR THESE TREES!

Banyan tree

The crown of the banyan tree named
Thimmamma Marrimanu, which is sacred
to the people of India, covers more ground
than two soccer stadiums!
**How did it manage to get so big
without falling over?**

SECONDARY TRUNKS GROW DOWNWARD
FROM THE HORIZONTAL BRANCHES,
HELPING TO SUPPORT THE CROWN.

THE BROADEST CROWN

**AN ENTIRE FOREST MADE UP
OF JUST ONE TREE!**

Quaking aspen

Experts have discovered that, in the United
States, there's an entire forest that's made
of just one tree! It's called Pando.
How, you're wondering?

A RECORD-SETTING FOREST

A SINGLE QUAKING ASPEN MANAGED TO
GENERATE NOT JUST ONE, BUT MANY
TRUNKS, UNTIL IT FORMED AN ENTIRE
FOREST MADE UP OF THE SAME PLANT.

ROOTS

The part of the tree that we can't see is probably the most important! Indeed, tree roots do three very fundamental things. They make it possible to **anchor the tree firmly to the ground**, so that it can grow upward without falling, and they **find and absorb water and nutrients from the soil**. They also constitute a **sensory organ**, which provides very important information about the environment to the tree.

HOW DO THEY DO ALL THAT?

The younger part of the roots is covered by special structures called **root hairs**. They extend into the ground, greatly increasing the surface of the roots and the ability of the tree to absorb nutrients and interact with other organisms, like fungi and animals underground.

SORT OF LIKE A BRAIN!

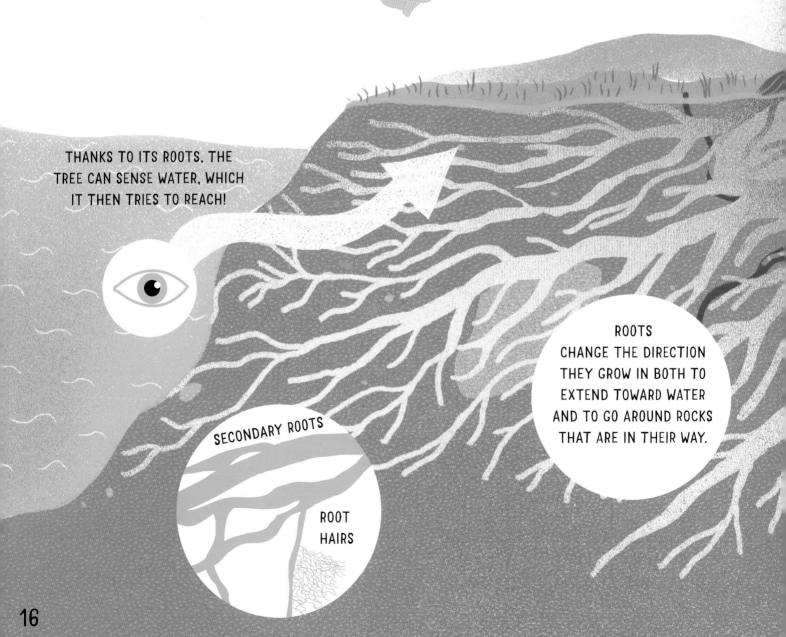

THANKS TO ITS ROOTS, THE TREE CAN SENSE WATER, WHICH IT THEN TRIES TO REACH!

ROOTS CHANGE THE DIRECTION THEY GROW IN BOTH TO EXTEND TOWARD WATER AND TO GO AROUND ROCKS THAT ARE IN THEIR WAY.

SECONDARY ROOTS

ROOT HAIRS

ROOT HAIRS MAKE IT POSSIBLE FOR THE TREE TO INTERACT WITH OTHER ORGANISMS.

HOW BIG ARE THE ROOTS OF A TREE? THEY CAN SOMETIMES TAKE UP A SPACE THAT'S EVEN BIGGER THAN THE TREE'S CROWN!

ARE ROOTS ALWAYS FOUND UNDERGROUND? NO! THERE ARE A FEW EXCEPTIONS!

TURN THE PAGE TO LEARN ABOUT THREE OF THEM!

UNIQUE ROOTS

Depending on the species, the climate, and the surrounding environment, roots can change shape and even leave the ground!

HERE ARE THREE EXAMPLES OF ROOTS THAT DO REALLY STRANGE THINGS!

AERIAL ROOTS

In some trees that grow in tropical areas, **special roots grow from the branches**. They are called "aerial" roots, and they latch on to their neighbors so that the tree can grow taller than them.

RECORD-BREAKING STRENGTH!

HAVE YOU EVER SEEN TREE ROOTS
THAT BREAK THE PAVEMENT IN A CITY?
HOW COULD A TREE DESTROY
SUCH A HARD, TOUGH MATERIAL?

Roots will extend into any small space they can, **in search of water** and nutrients. Once they've "taken root," they begin **to grow in diameter**, which is how, as time passes, they manage to break rocks, bend gates, and even lift asphalt!

ROOTS ARE REALLY STRONG!

UNDERWATER ROOTS

In **mangrove** forests, there are trees that live along the seashore, where they create forests floating above the water.

THESE SPECIAL ROOTS ANCHOR TREES TO THE GROUND WHILE OFTEN BEING ENTIRELY UNDERWATER DURING HIGH TIDE. THEY MAKE IT POSSIBLE FOR THE TREES TO SURVIVE EVEN IN SALTWATER.

MANGROVES ARE THE HABITAT OF MANY DIFFERENT ANIMALS, FROM FISH TO AMPHIBIANS, FROM REPTILES TO BIRDS.

THE TRUNK

The trunk is the part of the tree that grows upward and that **supports the branches and leaves**. It's also a conduit for **the transportation of water** and the nutrients absorbed and produced in every part of the plant. It works like a small freeway, made up of tiny channels through which the substances constantly circulate.

The trunk also stores the tree's **reserves**, which are to be used in times of hardship, such as in winter or in very hot summers.

WHAT'S THE TRUNK LIKE ON THE INSIDE?

If you look at a cross-section of a trunk, you'll notice **concentric rings** made of wood, which is the tissue that transports water and minerals from the ground to the top of the tree.

Each tree produces rings, which are formed on the outer layer of the trunk, allowing it to grow not only in height but also in width. By counting the rings of a trunk, you can discover how old a tree is. Try it on the opposite page!

INSIDE THE TRUNK

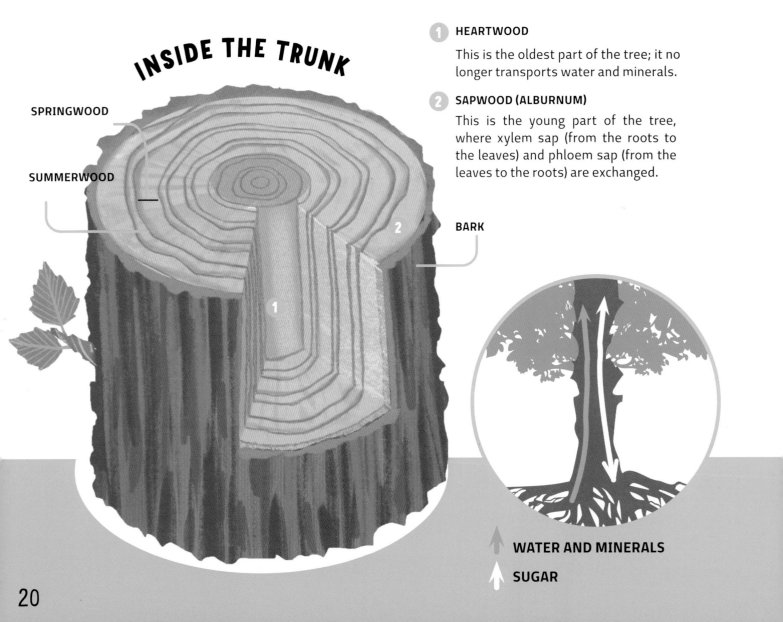

SPRINGWOOD

SUMMERWOOD

1 HEARTWOOD
This is the oldest part of the tree; it no longer transports water and minerals.

2 SAPWOOD (ALBURNUM)
This is the young part of the tree, where xylem sap (from the roots to the leaves) and phloem sap (from the leaves to the roots) are exchanged.

BARK

WATER AND MINERALS

SUGAR

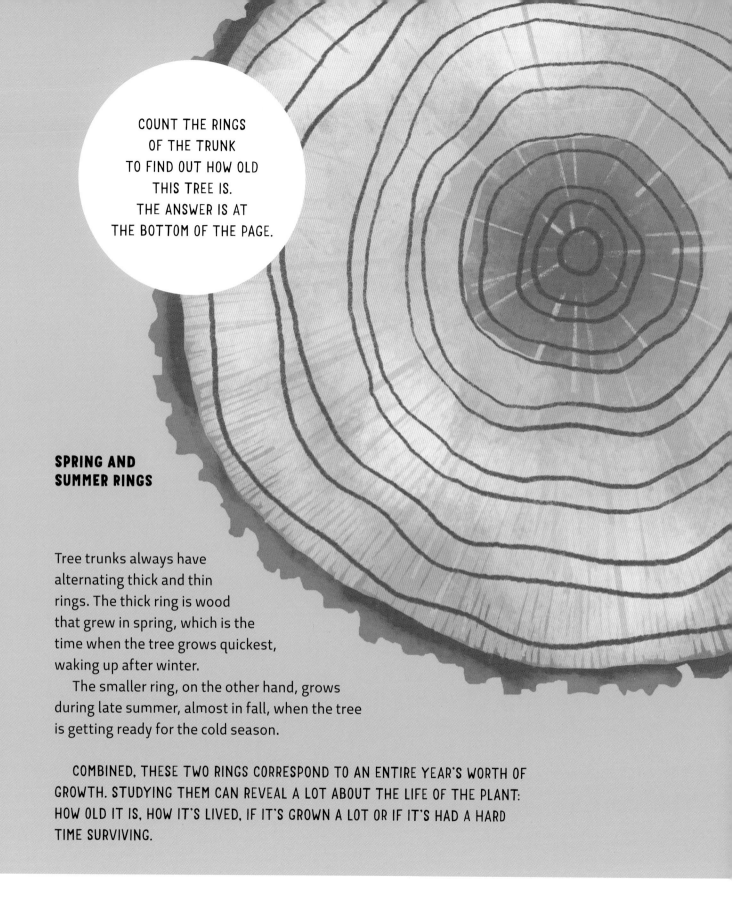

COUNT THE RINGS
OF THE TRUNK
TO FIND OUT HOW OLD
THIS TREE IS.
THE ANSWER IS AT
THE BOTTOM OF THE PAGE.

SPRING AND SUMMER RINGS

Tree trunks always have alternating thick and thin rings. The thick ring is wood that grew in spring, which is the time when the tree grows quickest, waking up after winter.

The smaller ring, on the other hand, grows during late summer, almost in fall, when the tree is getting ready for the cold season.

COMBINED, THESE TWO RINGS CORRESPOND TO AN ENTIRE YEAR'S WORTH OF GROWTH. STUDYING THEM CAN REVEAL A LOT ABOUT THE LIFE OF THE PLANT: HOW OLD IT IS, HOW IT'S LIVED, IF IT'S GROWN A LOT OR IF IT'S HAD A HARD TIME SURVIVING.

DENDROCHRONOLOGY: the science of studying the age of trees, made up of Greek words: *dendron* = tree, and *khronos* = time.

THIS TREE IS 13 YEARS OLD.

BARK

BARK IS A SORT OF "SKIN" FOR TREES: it helps protect them from the outside world and from predators, and it keeps them from losing water when it gets hot.

If you look at bark up close, you'll notice an element that all bark shares: a repeated pattern, whether it's formed by little dots, or by vertical or horizontal incisions, which can be deep or shallow.

BUT NOT ALL BARK IS THE SAME!

It can be thick or thin, or have deep cracks or wrinkles. On some trees, the bark comes off in thin pieces that almost look like leaves, while others have stinging thorns or even take on different colors.

HERE ARE A FEW EXAMPLES OF INCREDIBLE BARK!

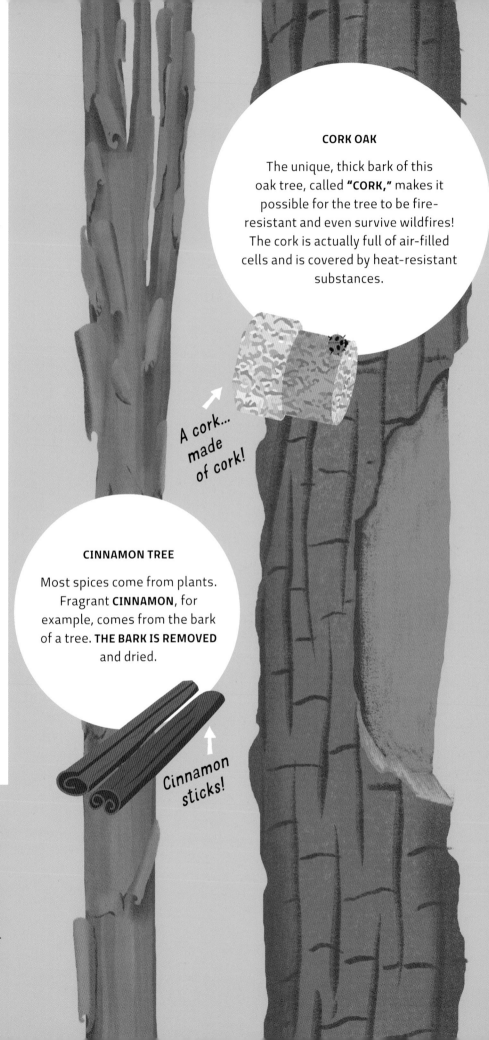

CORK OAK

The unique, thick bark of this oak tree, called **"CORK,"** makes it possible for the tree to be fire-resistant and even survive wildfires! The cork is actually full of air-filled cells and is covered by heat-resistant substances.

A cork... made of cork!

CINNAMON TREE

Most spices come from plants. Fragrant **CINNAMON**, for example, comes from the bark of a tree. **THE BARK IS REMOVED** and dried.

Cinnamon sticks!

WILLOW TREE
What makes this tree's bark unique is invisible, but really important!
In the late 1800s, some chemists discovered that the bark of the willow tree (of the genus *Salix*) contains *salicylic acid*, used in many medicines up to the modern day.

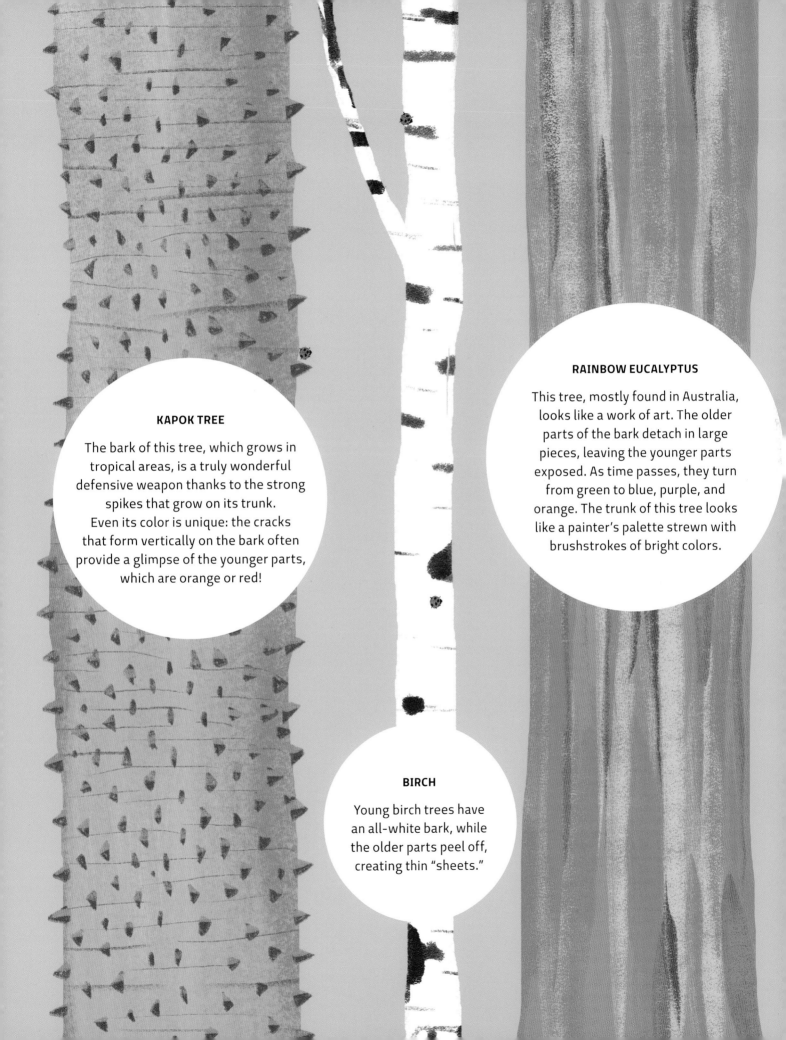

KAPOK TREE

The bark of this tree, which grows in tropical areas, is a truly wonderful defensive weapon thanks to the strong spikes that grow on its trunk.
Even its color is unique: the cracks that form vertically on the bark often provide a glimpse of the younger parts, which are orange or red!

RAINBOW EUCALYPTUS

This tree, mostly found in Australia, looks like a work of art. The older parts of the bark detach in large pieces, leaving the younger parts exposed. As time passes, they turn from green to blue, purple, and orange. The trunk of this tree looks like a painter's palette strewn with brushstrokes of bright colors.

BIRCH

Young birch trees have an all-white bark, while the older parts peel off, creating thin "sheets."

LEAVES

The leaf is the organ that helps plants get nourishment and breathe, thanks to a process that's called **PHOTOSYNTHESIS*.** Even if leaves can come in thousands of different shapes, they're all characterized by a few essential parts.

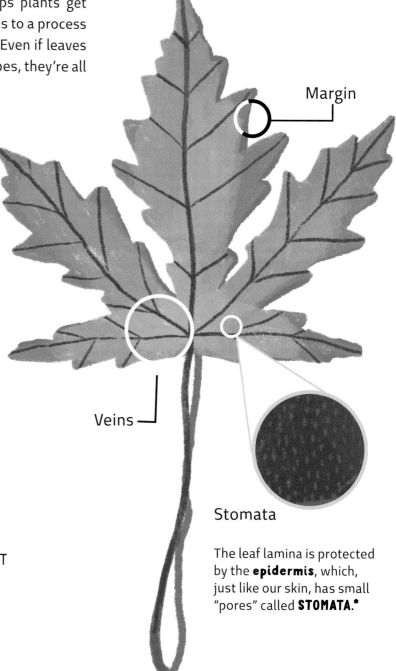

Margin

Veins

Stomata

LEAF PARTS

The **lamina** is the largest part of the leaf. It includes all the green surface and is rich in chlorophyll, which is necessary for **photosynthesis** to take place.

The outer edge of the leaves is called **margin**.

Leaves are crossed by "channels" that are called **"veins"**: just like human veins, they transport the nutritional substances produced by the leaves to the rest of the tree, and water and minerals from the roots to the leaves.

EVERY SPECIES HAS A PRECISE ARRANGEMENT OF THESE VEINS, MAKING THEM UNIQUE, JUST LIKE A FINGERPRINT!

The leaf lamina is protected by the **epidermis**, which, just like our skin, has small "pores" called **STOMATA.***

🍃 **PHOTOSYNTHESIS:** this is a process that takes place in plant cells and by which, starting from **WATER** and a gas called **CARBON DIOXIDE**, **SUGAR** and **OXYGEN** are produced. **To learn more, go to page 34.**

🍃 **STOMATA:** these small adjustable openings are used **FOR THE EXCHANGE OF GASES, SUCH AS CARBON DIOXIDE AND OXYGEN.**
These "pores" open according to the availability of water: when the plant is thirsty, the stomata are closed to ensure that water doesn't evaporate from them.

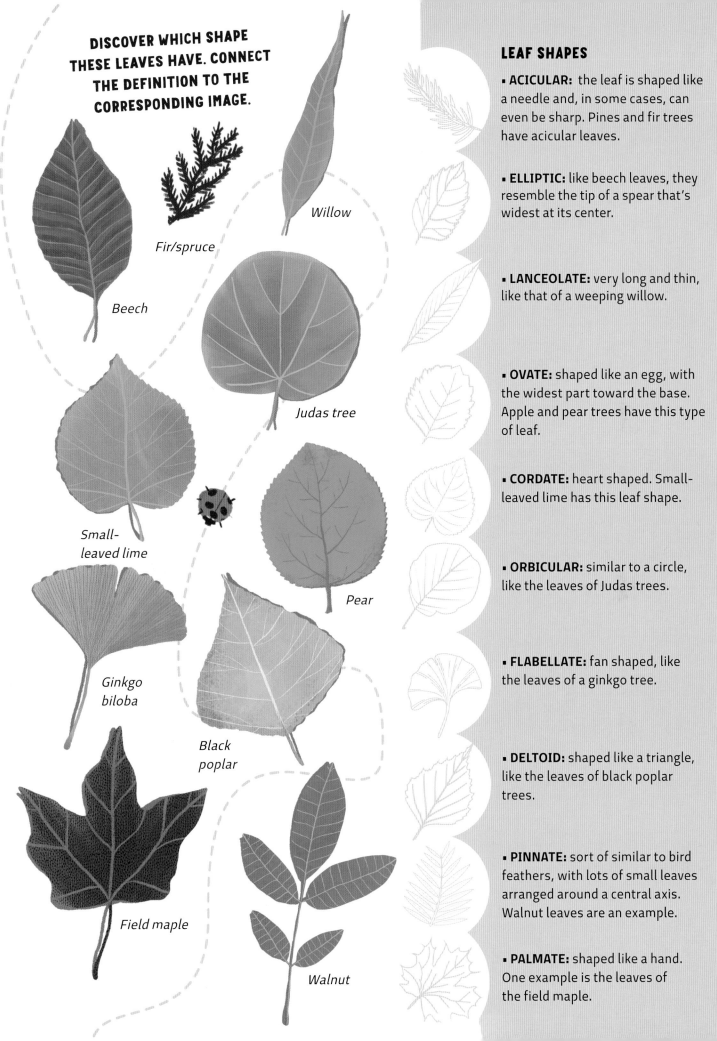

DISCOVER WHICH SHAPE THESE LEAVES HAVE. CONNECT THE DEFINITION TO THE CORRESPONDING IMAGE.

Fir/spruce

Willow

Beech

Judas tree

Small-leaved lime

Pear

Ginkgo biloba

Black poplar

Field maple

Walnut

LEAF SHAPES

- **ACICULAR:** the leaf is shaped like a needle and, in some cases, can even be sharp. Pines and fir trees have acicular leaves.

- **ELLIPTIC:** like beech leaves, they resemble the tip of a spear that's widest at its center.

- **LANCEOLATE:** very long and thin, like that of a weeping willow.

- **OVATE:** shaped like an egg, with the widest part toward the base. Apple and pear trees have this type of leaf.

- **CORDATE:** heart shaped. Small-leaved lime has this leaf shape.

- **ORBICULAR:** similar to a circle, like the leaves of Judas trees.

- **FLABELLATE:** fan shaped, like the leaves of a ginkgo tree.

- **DELTOID:** shaped like a triangle, like the leaves of black poplar trees.

- **PINNATE:** sort of similar to bird feathers, with lots of small leaves arranged around a central axis. Walnut leaves are an example.

- **PALMATE:** shaped like a hand. One example is the leaves of the field maple.

EXCEPTIONAL LEAVES

Every tree has a typical leaf shape specific to that species, but there are exceptions!

HOW MANY TREES DO THESE THREE LEAVES BELONG TO?

JUST ONE: THE MULBERRY TREE!

Black mulberry trees can have **differently shaped leaves, even on the same branch**. This truly strange quality doesn't seem to exist for any particular reason.

For holly oaks, on the other hand, having different leaves **is an essential defense mechanism**: the leaves on the lower branches, nibbled on by grazing animals, regrow but with spikes along their edges.

THIS PHENOMENA IS CALLED "HETEROPHYLLY."*

HOLLY OAK

ACACIAS, FOR EXAMPLE,
HAVE LONG SPIKES
ALONG THEIR BRANCHES
TO DETER HERBIVORES
INTENT ON EATING
THEIR LEAVES.

**OTHER LEAVES CHANGE THEIR SHAPE...
TO ATTRACT ANIMALS!**

Flower petals are none other than modified leaves: instead of green chlorophyll, they're rich in colorful pigments to attract pollinating insects and animals.

HETEROPHYLLY: this word derives from Greek: *hetero* = different and *phyllia* = leaf.
It indicates the presence of differently shaped leaves on the same plant, which occurs as a response to environmental stimuli. Examples include a defense mechanism from predators or in response to different sun exposure, or as an inherent trait of the species that isn't connected to external factors.

THE SEASONAL CYCLE

When it starts to get **cold** and the days get shorter, that means that fall is about to start, and the leaves of many trees begin to change color. Up until a few days prior, those same leaves perhaps were a **bright shade of green**! They turn **brown**, **yellow**, **orange**, or **red**, and then fall off their branches, marking the end of the seasonal cycle of the tree.

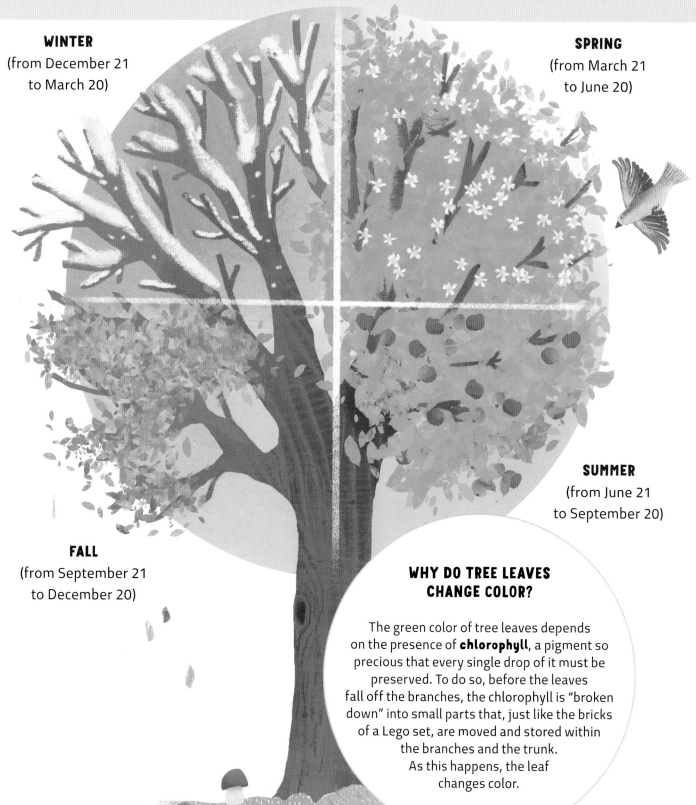

WINTER
(from December 21
to March 20)

SPRING
(from March 21
to June 20)

SUMMER
(from June 21
to September 20)

FALL
(from September 21
to December 20)

WHY DO TREE LEAVES CHANGE COLOR?

The green color of tree leaves depends on the presence of **chlorophyll**, a pigment so precious that every single drop of it must be preserved. To do so, before the leaves fall off the branches, the chlorophyll is "broken down" into small parts that, just like the bricks of a Lego set, are moved and stored within the branches and the trunk. As this happens, the leaf changes color.

28

SPRING IS COMING!

In **spring**, when the tree "wakes up," **new leaves** appear from **buds**: they've been there all **winter**, waiting for the right time to emerge and grow.

THE SIGNAL THAT LETS THEM KNOW IT'S TIME IS THE INCREASING AMOUNT OF DAYLIGHT, RISING TEMPERATURES, AND THE INCREASED AMOUNT OF WATER FROM SPRING RAINFALL OR MELTING SNOW.

EVERGREEN TREES INCLUDE FIR, SPRUCE, PINE, CYPRESS, HOLLY OAK, AND OLIVE TREES.

EVERGREEN TREES

Some trees, called **evergreens**, keep their leaves even in winter. Some examples are **conifers** and many species that live around the Mediterranean.

DO THESE TREES LOSE THEIR LEAVES? WHEN?

Evergreen trees cyclically replace their leaves **during the entire year**, changing them when they get old. The leaves of these trees thus don't all fall at the same time, which is why we never see them completely bare.

CHAPTER 2

THE LIVES OF TREES

What do people and trees have in common and what makes them different?

Let's discover how they are "born"; what they eat; how they reproduce, breathe, move, and even "talk"; and how they get sick and die.

HOW IS A TREE BORN?

Every tree is unique, but they all are "born" in the same way: they sprout from **a seed**.

Within each seed is a tiny tree that's sleeping, waiting for a **sign** that lets it know it's time to wake up. Some seeds react to moisture, some to light, and others to temperature.

WHERE ARE SEEDS FOUND?

Fruit is the part of the tree that holds the seed. Its purpose is to help **spread its seeds** and thus make it possible for trees to **reproduce**.

THROUGH THE SEEDS IN THEIR FRUIT, NEW SPECIMENS OF TREES CAN CROP UP EVEN AT GREAT DISTANCES, THANKS TO INCREDIBLE STRATEGIES. HERE ARE A FEW.

STINKY SEEDS!

The seeds of the **baobab** are stored in **fruit** that elephants just love to eat.

As the fruit is digested, the thick layer around the seed is removed, and after being expelled as feces, the seed finally reaches the soil.

WITHOUT THIS FOUL-SMELLING PROCESS, SEEDS WOULDN'T BE ABLE TO GERMINATE!

IT FLOATS LIKE A BOAT!

FLOATING SEEDS

Coconuts, the fruit of certain palms, have a very hard shell that's full of **air** on the inside: these characteristics make it possible for them to **float** on the sea's currents. They can travel long distances before they reach a beach and sprout into a new palm tree.

WARNING! SEED EXPLOSION IN 3, 2, 1...

EXPLODING SEEDS

The fruit of the tropical *Hura crepitans* tree is famous for its ability to **explode**!

When the fruit is ripe, it suddenly explodes, managing to scatter its seeds up to **330 ft (100 m) away**! As such, the tree can reach places that are quite far from its crown, without having to rely on animals or the wind.

FRUIT ARMOR

The pine cones of the Swiss pine tree hold their seeds, which we call "pine nuts." They **never open**, not even when ripe!
So, how do the seeds get out?

A bird called the **spotted nutcracker** uses its strong beak to poke a hole in the pine cone to reach the seeds and eat them. When winter draws near, however, the bird buries them in the ground as a sort of food stockpile. Not all pine nuts are later found by the nutcracker, and they remain in the ground, ready to turn into a new pine tree!

FLYING SEEDS

With a **lightweight propeller**, these seeds are transported by the wind, twirling about like a helicopter or gliding along the ground like a hang-glider, until they land far away.

SPOTTED NUTCRACKER

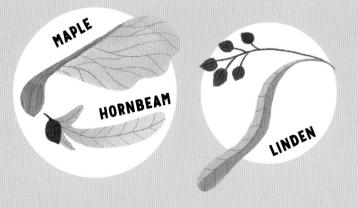

MAPLE

HORNBEAM

LINDEN

REPRODUCTION STRATEGIES

To make sure that the tree produces a seed and the fruit that holds it, **POLLINATION** must take place.* In nature, this can happen in a number of different ways.

Some trees allow pollen granules to be carried by the wind, using a type of pollination called **anemophily**.

Other species prefer to get a little help from animals: this type of pollination, called **zoophilic** or **zoogamous,** involves insects or even other animals such as birds and bats.

FLOWER PETALS HAVE COLORS AND HUES THAT ARE VISIBLE ONLY TO ANIMALS THAT, DUE TO THEIR CHARACTERISTICS, HELP THE PLANT BE POLLINATED MORE THAN OTHERS!

WHAT BEES SEE!

HOW DO PLANTS GET ANIMALS TO HELP THEM AT THIS IMPORTANT MOMENT?

To get animals to help them, plants offer a sort of **reward**. Flowers, for example, produce the **nectar** that **insect pollinators** eat.

As it moves along the surface of the flower in search of nectar, the plant's **pollen** sticks to the body of the insect. The insect flies from flower to flower, pollinating them.

FROM POLLEN TO FRUIT

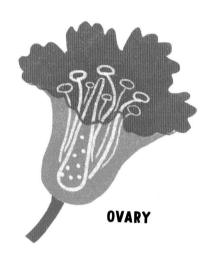

OVARY

ONCE POLLINATION HAS TAKEN PLACE, A TRANSFORMATION BEGINS TO TAKE PLACE IN THE FLOWER: SEEDS AND FRUIT BEGIN TO FORM.

1 These important events take place in the **ovary**, which is the part of the flower that will grow into fruit.

2 After pollination and fertilization, the petals and stamens begin to wilt. This is because once they've attracted insects, their purpose has come to an end.

POLLINATION: the transport of pollen from the male to female parts of the plant. It's the action that makes fertilization and seed development possible.

WHAT DO TREES EAT?

Trees are **autotrophs**. That means they are organisms that can produce the nutrients they need on their own, thanks to processes such as **photosynthesis,** which makes it possible for them to generate the sugar that is essential to their survival.

HOWEVER, THERE ARE OTHER SUBSTANCES THAT ARE INDISPENSABLE TO TREES.

Tree roots absorb water, but also **mineral salts** and **nitrogen**, which they need to create chlorophyll. To find these substances, trees have learned to **collaborate** with other organisms. That includes fungi, which are often found near their root hairs. Do you remember what those are? We talked about them on page 16.

RAYS OF THE SUN

CARBON DIOXIDE

GLUCOSE

WATER AND MINERALS

PHOTOSYNTHESIS

Photosynthesis is a complex process that takes place in plant leaves and turns solar energy into sugar, called "**glucose**," which is the main food source of the plant.

In order for photosynthesis to occur, there needs to be **water** absorbed by the roots and then carried to the leaves. There, **chlorophyll** uses the **energy** of the **sun** to combine the water with **carbon dioxide**, producing glucose.

WHAT IS THE GLUCOSE PRODUCED VIA PHOTOSYNTHESIS USED FOR?

It can be distributed throughout the entire tree as nourishment, or it can be **used to create specific tree parts, such as fruit**, whose sweet flavor is determined by the presence of this exact sugar!

The tree might also turn glucose into **CELLULOSE***, a molecule that's essential to generating wood and supporting the overall growth of the tree.

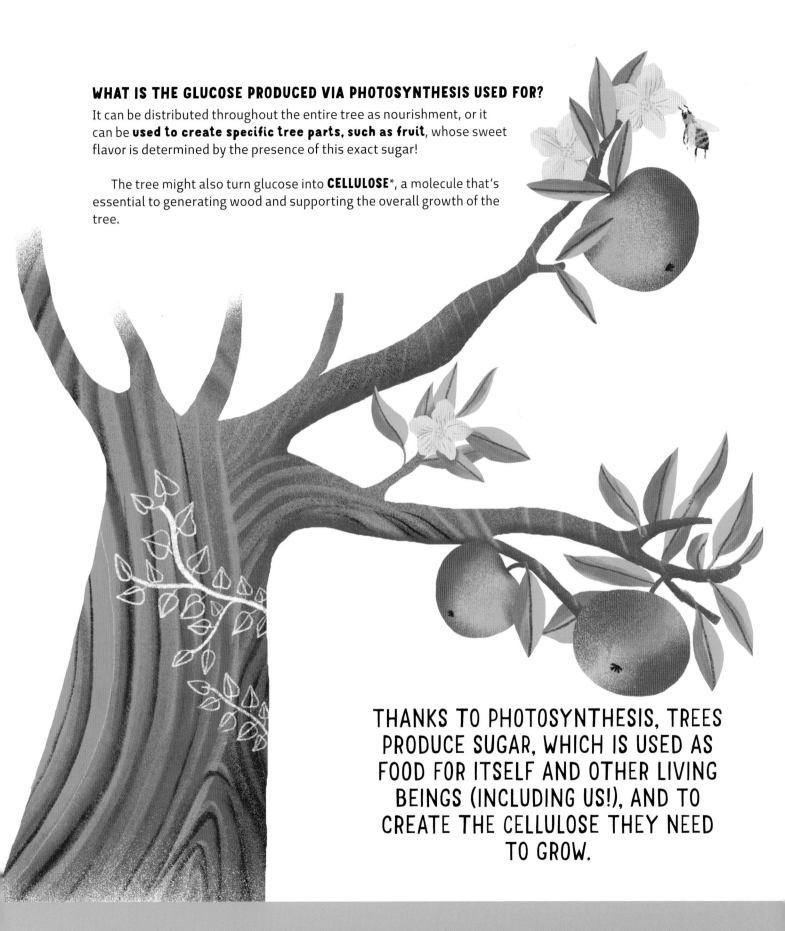

THANKS TO PHOTOSYNTHESIS, TREES PRODUCE SUGAR, WHICH IS USED AS FOOD FOR ITSELF AND OTHER LIVING BEINGS (INCLUDING US!), AND TO CREATE THE CELLULOSE THEY NEED TO GROW.

CELLULOSE: a very important molecule found in every tree cell. Like a sort of scaffolding, cellulose helps cells hold their shape. Thanks to cellulose, trees can grow upward without falling and produce new leaves and roots.

CAN TREES BREATHE?

During **photosynthesis**, oxygen is released into the air. We need this gas to breathe, as do other animals and even the trees themselves!

HOW DO TREES BREATHE?

Trees, unlike animals and humans, do not need lungs to allow air to enter and gases to be exchanged, because the oxygen they need is absorbed from their surroundings through their leaves, roots, and trunk. Trees even produce oxygen themselves through photosynthesis.

Like other living beings, trees need oxygen for a fundamental process called **CELLULAR RESPIRATION***.

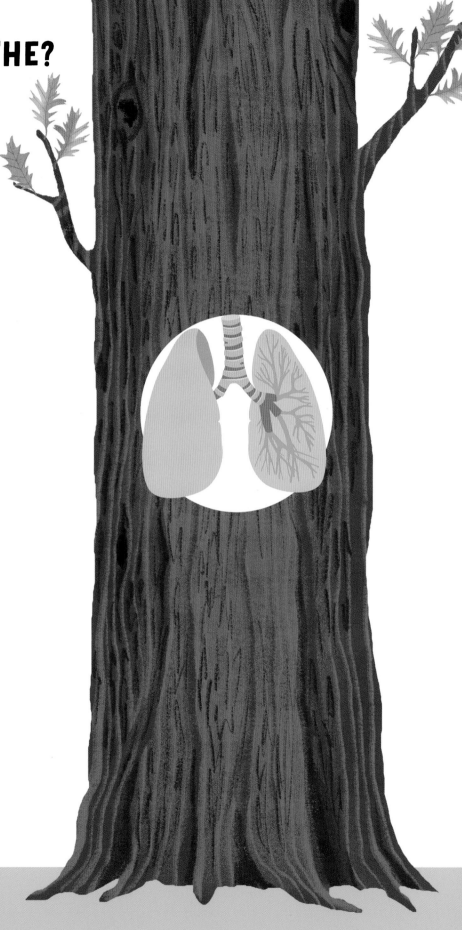

*CELLULAR RESPIRATION: a process that takes place in plant and animal cells and that is required to produce energy, starting from sugar and oxygen. Trees use this energy for all vital functions, including growing and developing new roots, branches, and leaves.

HOW DO TREES MOVE?

Trees can't really move, but they are able to make movements, albeit slow and almost imperceptible to our eyes! The simplest of them is linked to the growth and movement of the leaves, which turn toward the sun. But it isn't the only one!

TREES HAVE DEVELOPED INCREDIBLE STRATEGIES FOR MOVEMENT. HERE ARE A FEW.

NEXT!

The forest never stops moving!
   When a tree falls or is cut down, the ones near it immediately start growing branches and leaves where that tree once stood. They do so to take advantage of the available space and light.

PROFITEERING TREES

Some trees are really very fast...at growing. In tropical areas, some types of *Ficus* grow by using **other trees as a base**, resting on them so that they can exceed them in height and spread their branches and leaves out above the older tree.

COLONIZING TREES

The most common way for trees to move is through their **fruit and seeds** (as we saw on page 31).

AS THEY DO, TREES TAKE OVER NEW SPACES, COLONIZING NEW LANDS AND CREATING FORESTS WHERE THERE WERE NONE.

HOW DO TREES FIGHT?

In nature, every organism competes with others to survive, including trees. They battle over **light**, **water**, **nutrients**, and **space**.

HOW DO TREES FIGHT?
HERE ARE THREE EXAMPLES.

COMPETING FOR SUNLIGHT

Taller trees cast shade over smaller ones below them, limiting their ability to carry out photosynthesis. Nevertheless, the shorter trees have learned to adapt to less light, producing **bigger leaves**.

COMPETING FOR SPACE

Some species, like walnut or peach trees, can limit the growth of other plants by **spreading chemical substances** in the ground, thereby slowing or even inhibiting the growth of nearby plants. Thanks to this strategy, there is always a lot of space all around them!

COMPETING FOR WATER

Trees compete for water and nutrients in the soil through their roots: those with the deepest or most extensive root networks can **more easily reach the ground's resources** compared to nearby trees with less developed root systems.

HOW DO TREES COMMUNICATE?

Trees are able to communicate even if they don't speak and they can't move! They **exchange important information with nearby trees and with organisms found in the ecosystem**. For example, they can warn the trees around them of danger such as harmful insects or diseases, allowing them to activate self-defense mechanisms.

Trees communicate with each other through a **language that we are unable to decipher**. Tree "words" are actually chemical molecules that are emitted **through their roots**.

TREES DON'T ONLY COMMUNICATE THROUGH THEIR ROOTS!

THE SECRET MESSAGES OF LEAVES

Another way that trees communicate is through their **leaves**: when a tree gets attacked by predators, its leaves release special molecules into the air. The nearby trees are thus warned about the enemy presence.

That sets off **a chain reaction of communication and defense** throughout the entire forest!

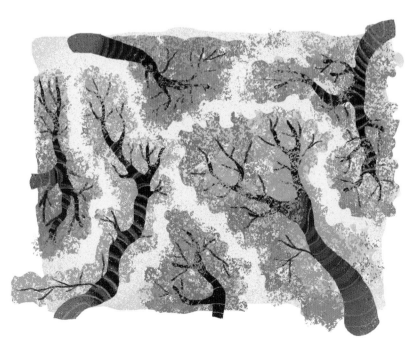

SHY TREE CROWNS

If we were to look at a forest of *Dryobalanops aromatica* from above, we would notice that the crowns of these trees aren't touching!

Experts think that this unique behavior is designed to reduce the spread of parasites from one tree to another.

In this case, the lack of communication helps the forest survive.

WOOD WIDE WEB (TREE NETWORKS)

Like the internet (the World Wide Web), trees also create connections with their kind...and beyond! Fungi, with their ultra-fine underground filaments (called **hyphae**), give life to true networks that make the exchange of information and nutrients possible.

WHY DO FUNGI HELP TREES?

Because trees help fungi in return! When they provide nutrients to the tree, the tree then releases sugar that is useful to the fungi. The exchange between the roots of the tree and the hyphae of the fungi is continuous. They therefore develop a very close relationship, sort of like a friendship bond, in true **SYMBIOSIS.***

THIS RELATIONSHIP IS CALLED "MYCORRHIZA."

GOOD FUNGI (FOR THE TREES)

SYMBIOSIS: an association between two or more organisms of different species that gives rise to shared benefits and advantages.

THE SOIL IS ALIVE!

HAVE YOU EVER THOUGHT ABOUT THE SOIL AND ALL THAT IT HIDES?

Soil is one of the most complex systems on our planet. It is the result of the breakdown of rocks by living beings and the weather, and the decomposition of plants and animals.

BAD FUNGI
(FOR THE TREES)

There are also parasitic fungi that steal nourishment from trees, without providing anything in exchange.

THE SOIL IS HOME TO LOTS OF DIFFERENT ORGANISMS, WHICH ENSURE THE CONTINUOUS TRANSFORMATION OF THE NOURISHMENT ABSORBED BY THE TREES.

HYPHAE

IN A HANDFUL OF SOIL, THERE ARE ABOUT 31 MILES (50 KM) OF HYPHAE.

HOW LONG DO TREES LIVE?

On average, the lifespan of a tree is longer than that of a human.

One of the secrets to their long life is their ability to regenerate their body parts, potentially forever, whenever they are damaged or harmed.

Like other plants, trees are made up of **many similar parts that are repeated and that can be substituted**, such as roots or leaves. This characteristic allows trees to **easily adapt to different environmental conditions**, which may also change quite quickly. It makes it possible for them to adapt and survive, even if they can't move, migrate, or run away like many animals can.

LIFE IN SLOW MOTION!
The lifespan of a tree doesn't depend on its size, but on how fast it grows and on its structure. Bristlecone pines and olive trees, **some of the longest-living** trees in the world, grow very slowly. It's as if time, for them, is moving in **slow motion** compared to us!

POPLARS ARE SUPER FAST!

This tree grows very **quickly**. For that reason, its wood is less dense and is lighter than that of trees that grow more slowly. This characteristic exposes poplars to attacks by fungi and insects, the main cause of their death.

However, the quick growth of poplars makes them a favorite among people: poplars are grown for the production of **paper** because their wood can be harvested after just a few years.

TO DISCOVER OTHER WAYS IN WHICH TREES CAN HELP PEOPLE, SEE PAGE 56.

DO TREES SUFFER? AND HOW DO THEY DEFEND THEMSELVES?

Trees don't have a brain or nerves, so they can't feel **pain** like people can. But that doesn't mean they don't suffer in some ways.

TREE SCARS

When a tree is physically damaged, for example if it's cut or burned, it can **react** to protect itself and allow the wound to close, if not heal entirely.

A calloused area may form around the damaged area, made of thicker, tougher wood that blocks the infiltration of pathogens and harmful organisms. It's as if the tree forms a sort of **scar** that's thicker around the area to protect.

SCRAM!

Some trees, such as some *Ficus* and *Euphorbia* species, release a sort of white latex that contains substances that are irritants, repellents, or even toxic to some animals.

THANKS TO THIS ADAPTATION, THESE SPECIES ARE ABLE TO KEEP PREDATORS AWAY, BLOCKING THEIR ABILITY TO FURTHER DAMAGE THE PLANT.

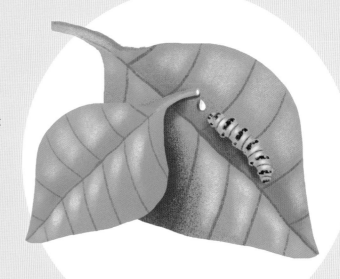

A NATURAL BAND-AID!

Within the trunks of conifers, which include fir and pine trees, there are channels that transport **resin**. When the trunk or a branch is damaged, the tree immediately releases a large quantity of this viscous, sticky substance.

RESIN IMMEDIATELY COVERS THE WOUND, ISOLATING IT FROM THE OUTSIDE OR FROM PREDATORS.

WHEN WE GET HURT, WE SCREAM, JUMP, RUN AWAY, OR COMPLAIN. TREES, ON THE OTHER HAND, SEEM TO REMAIN IMPASSIVE IN THE FACE OF ALL SORTS OF INJURIES: THIS DOESN'T MEAN, HOWEVER, THAT THEY DON'T SUFFER!

THE DEATH OF A TREE

Even trees are destined to die when they get old, weak, and thus less resistant to disease or environmental factors.

Some **harmful organisms**, such as fungi, bacteria, or viruses, can at that point spread easily within the tree, compromising its entire structure until it dies.
Even **the environment** can be dangerous! Strong winds or intense rainfall can break even the thickest branches of an old tree or cause irreparable harm that may lead to its death. Moreover, climate change, such as unusually long periods of drought, can put entire forests at risk!

Forests are also threatened by **human activities**, such as deforestation or land grabbing for farming.

WHAT HAPPENS WHEN A TREE DIES IN A FOREST?

It's normal for trees to die, and it happens constantly in forests. Actually, it helps keep forests healthy, guaranteeing the presence of ever-new species and individuals.

Plus, **the remains of a fallen tree turn into a precious life resource for other organisms**, such as insects, fungi, bacteria, and even other plants, which use the wood to grow and develop.

LOOKING AT THE TRUNK OF A FALLEN TREE, YOU ALMOST CERTAINLY WILL FIND THE TRACES OF STAG BEETLES. THESE INSECTS LAY THEIR EGGS ON DEAD OR ROTTING WOOD, WHICH THEN IS EATEN BY THE LARVAE. THEY LIVE FOR YEARS, DIGGING LONG TUNNELS ON THE INSIDE OF DEAD TREES.

STAG BEETLE LARVAE

CHAPTER 3

TREES AND ANIMALS

For some animals, trees are a source of food. For others, they're a tried and true home!

In this chapter, you'll find lots of examples of relationships between trees and animals, and they often include solutions and adaptations that are really curious!

BIRDS AND NESTS

Many birds build their nests in trees, laying their eggs and raising their chicks in them. The elevated position of a nest in a tree makes it possible to avoid predators on land. But when even that isn't enough, birds adopt incredible nest construction strategies too. Here are five examples.

THEY'RE IMPRESSIVE ARCHITECTS!

Male **weaverbirds** build nests that are truly complex. Interweaving blades of grass and twigs, they create a structure that's a bit like an upside-down sack.

TO BROOD THE EGGS, THE NEST HAS ONE OR MORE SMALL "ROOMS," THE ENTRANCE TO WHICH, PLACED AT THE END OF A SMALL TUNNEL, CAN ONLY BE ACCESSED WHEN FLYING.

WHAT'S ALL THAT RACKET?!

The **sociable weaver** is a bird that lives in southern Africa that has learned to share its space with others of its species. Using blades of grass, it builds giant nests that take up a large part of the crown of a tree, creating a small bird village.

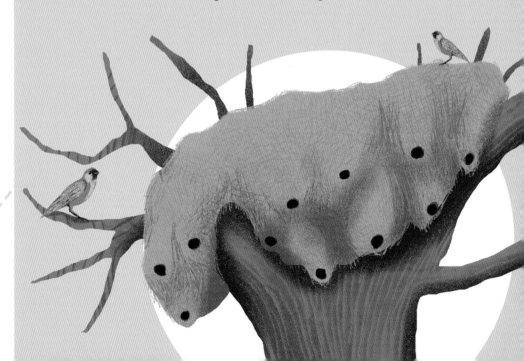

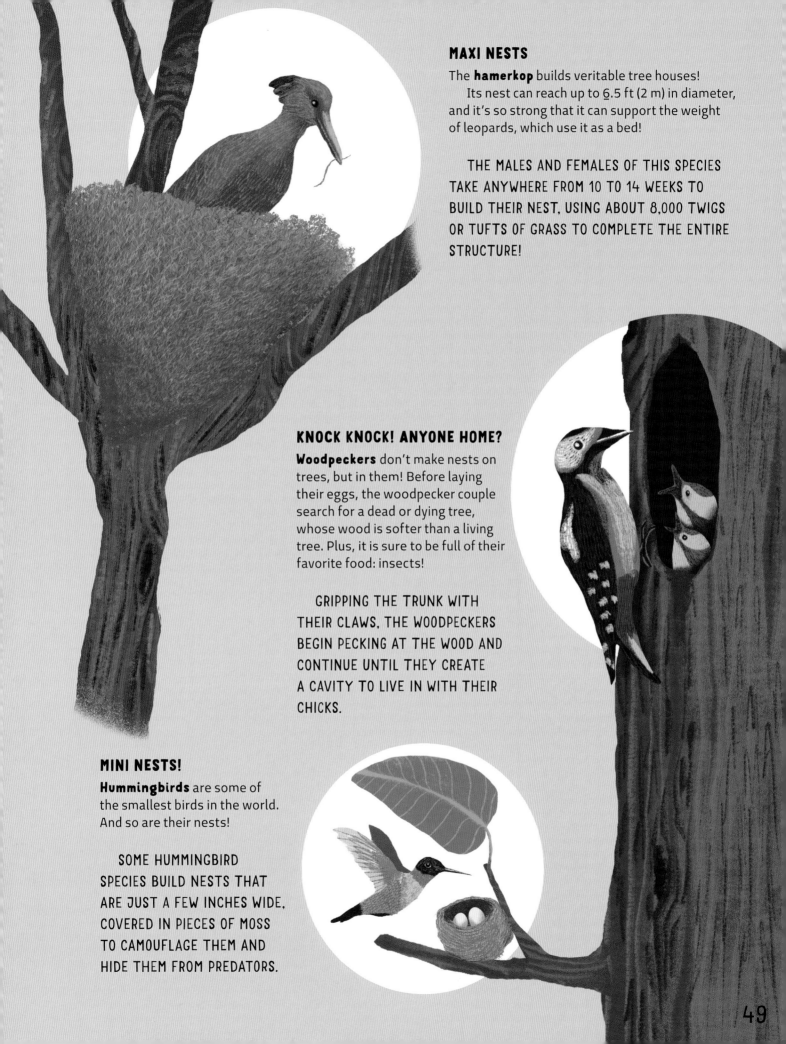

MAXI NESTS

The **hamerkop** builds veritable tree houses!
Its nest can reach up to 6.5 ft (2 m) in diameter, and it's so strong that it can support the weight of leopards, which use it as a bed!

THE MALES AND FEMALES OF THIS SPECIES TAKE ANYWHERE FROM 10 TO 14 WEEKS TO BUILD THEIR NEST, USING ABOUT 8,000 TWIGS OR TUFTS OF GRASS TO COMPLETE THE ENTIRE STRUCTURE!

KNOCK KNOCK! ANYONE HOME?

Woodpeckers don't make nests on trees, but in them! Before laying their eggs, the woodpecker couple search for a dead or dying tree, whose wood is softer than a living tree. Plus, it is sure to be full of their favorite food: insects!

GRIPPING THE TRUNK WITH THEIR CLAWS, THE WOODPECKERS BEGIN PECKING AT THE WOOD AND CONTINUE UNTIL THEY CREATE A CAVITY TO LIVE IN WITH THEIR CHICKS.

MINI NESTS!

Hummingbirds are some of the smallest birds in the world. And so are their nests!

SOME HUMMINGBIRD SPECIES BUILD NESTS THAT ARE JUST A FEW INCHES WIDE, COVERED IN PIECES OF MOSS TO CAMOUFLAGE THEM AND HIDE THEM FROM PREDATORS.

NOT JUST BIRDS!

In addition to birds, many other animals have learned to use trees as homes, even spending their entire lives up in their branches.

SLOTHS

Among the branches of trees, this animal finds not only a safe haven but also the fruit and leaves that make up its diet. Sloths descend from trees just once a week—to poop!

MALE SLOTHS LIVE THEIR ENTIRE LIFE UP IN THE SAME TREE, WHILE FEMALE SLOTHS MOVE TO A NEW TREE WHEN THEIR CUB IS BIG ENOUGH TO MAKE IT ON ITS OWN, LEAVING IT THE TREE IT WAS BORN IN.

AMPHIBIANS ARE WELCOME TOO!

Some frogs that live in tropical forests have learned to lay their eggs in trees! They take advantage of the special shape of some leaves, within which rainwater tends to collect. In these miniature lakes, floating amid the tree's branches, these frogs, and even tiny crustaceans and insects, have found their ideal environment.

50

SQUIRRELS AND DORMICE

Even squirrels spend a large percentage of their lives in trees, and, like talented tightrope walkers, they jump from one branch to the next with sudden movements to escape predators.

SQUIRRELS AND DORMICE ALSO USE TREES AS A PLACE TO SLEEP AT NIGHT: THEY MAKE COMFY DENS IN THE NATURAL HOLLOWS OF TRUNKS.

AN UNDERGROUND HOUSE

The collaboration between trees and animals also extends underground. In fact, many small mammals, such as hedgehogs, shrews, and wild rabbits, as well as reptiles, insects, and worms, find a safe place to live among tree roots.

INSECT FRIENDS AND...

As they fly from flower to flower, **insect pollinators**, such as bees, butterflies, and beetles, perform a very important task: they carry pollen and enable pollination (as discussed before, on page 32).

Without the help of insect pollinators, many trees would not survive, with enormous repercussions for the lives of animals and humans as well!

LET'S LEARN MORE ABOUT THREE OF THESE BIODIVERSITY CHAMPIONS!

BEES

Bees are the primary, most well-known pollinating insects. There are many species of them, besides the one that humans have learned to breed for **honey** (i.e., *Apis mellifera*).

BEE

CARPENTER BEE

These large bees lead a solitary life and do not build hives. Instead, they dig **small tunnels** in rotting wood, where they lay their eggs. They're dark in color and their wings have a purplish reflection, coloring that allows them to collect heat through solar radiation and to be one of the main pollinators active in spring.

CARPENTER BEE

LARGE EARTH BUMBLEBEE

This insect is larger than an ordinary bee.
Its body also is covered with soft down.
Bumblebees form **small colonies**, fewer in number
than common bees. When winter arrives, only the
queen bumblebee survives, which, in the following
spring, brings a new colony to life.

LARGE EARTH
BUMBLEBEE

HUMMINGBIRD
HAWK-MOTH

HUMMINGBIRD HAWK-MOTH

This very strange moth has small wings that it flaps very fast, which enables it to remain suspended in
the air in front of the flowers on which it feeds. Precisely because of its very rapid movements, it is called
a "hummingbird hawk-moth." Like all moths, it has a long **proboscis**, with which it can reach the nectar of
even the narrowest and longest flowers.

53

...INDUBITABLY UNWELCOME INSECTS!

Some animals, even extremely small ones, are a risk to the very health and existence of the trees they coexist with!

LEAFCUTTER ANTS

These insects live in Central and South America. The entire huge colony, consisting of thousands of unstoppable warrior ants, traverses the jungle in search of a tree from which to collect massive quantities of leaves. **With their powerful jaws, the ants cut and shred the tree's leaves**, which are then transported to their anthill in long, organized lines.

Why do they do it?

THE LEAVES PROVIDE NOURISHMENT FOR A SPECIAL FUNGUS THAT GROWS UNDERGROUND IN THEIR ANTHILL AND IN TURN FEEDS THE ENTIRE COLONY!

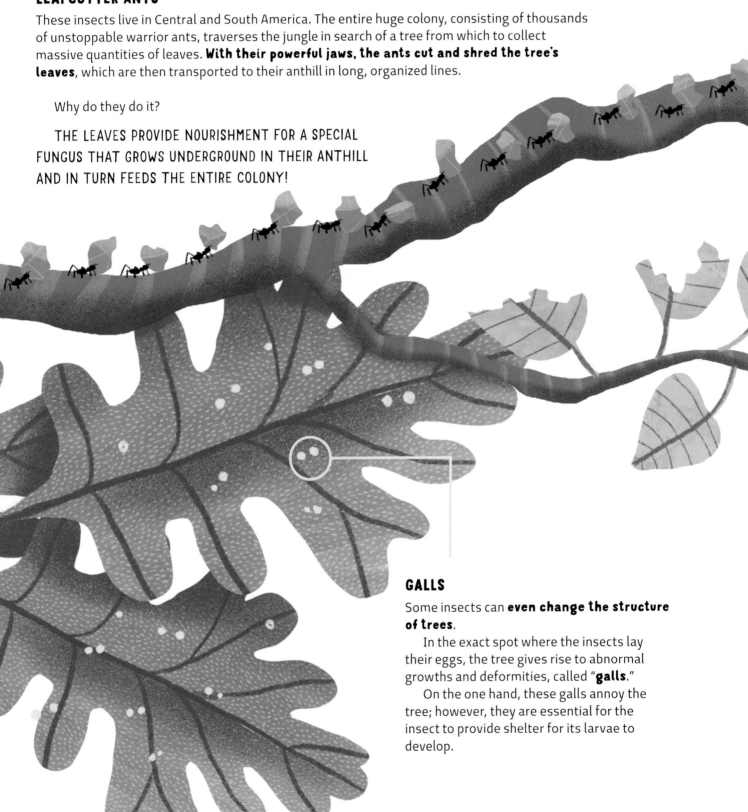

GALLS

Some insects can **even change the structure of trees**.

In the exact spot where the insects lay their eggs, the tree gives rise to abnormal growths and deformities, called "**galls**."

On the one hand, these galls annoy the tree; however, they are essential for the insect to provide shelter for its larvae to develop.

LEAFCUTTER ANTS ARE EVERY TROPICAL TREE'S NIGHTMARE!

NOT ONLY INSECTS. PLANTS TOO!

Some plants are able to parasitize trees to survive. One such example is mistletoe, which can grow on tree branches and trunks, penetrating within them.

IN FACT, THIS PLANT HAS SPECIAL ROOTS THAT "STEAL" WATER AND NUTRIENTS DIRECTLY FROM THE WOOD OF THE TREE.

MISTLETOE REACHES NEW TREES TO PARASITIZE THROUGH THE DROPPINGS OF BIRDS WHO LOVE TO EAT THE FRUIT OF THIS PLANT, MAKING THEM UNKNOWING ALLIES!

CHAPTER 4

TREES AND HUMAN BEINGS

With their majestic, silent presence, trees have stood alongside humanity since time immemorial.

Over the centuries, we have learned not only how to use trees in a variety of areas of everyday life, but we have also learned how and why they are indispensable to our own survival, and that of the planet!

TREES PROTECT...

We can consider trees to be true defenders of life on our planet. Here are four examples that show how indispensable their presence is.

...THE AIR WE BREATHE

As we learned already (on page 34), as a result of photosynthesis, **trees and other plants release oxygen**, a gas that we need to breathe. Interestingly, this process is triggered by the absorption of another gas, carbon dioxide, a molecule whose overabundance is one of the causes of climate change.*

Without trees, the quality of the air we breathe would be reduced and global warming would be even more severe.

FORESTS CAN BE CONSIDERED
LARGE AIR "PURIFIERS,"
THE HUGE LUNGS OF OUR PLANET.

...LIFE ON EARTH

Trees and forests preserve biodiversity and the many forms of life that inhabit the earth. **Without them, there would be no home for many animals**, fungi, and other plants.

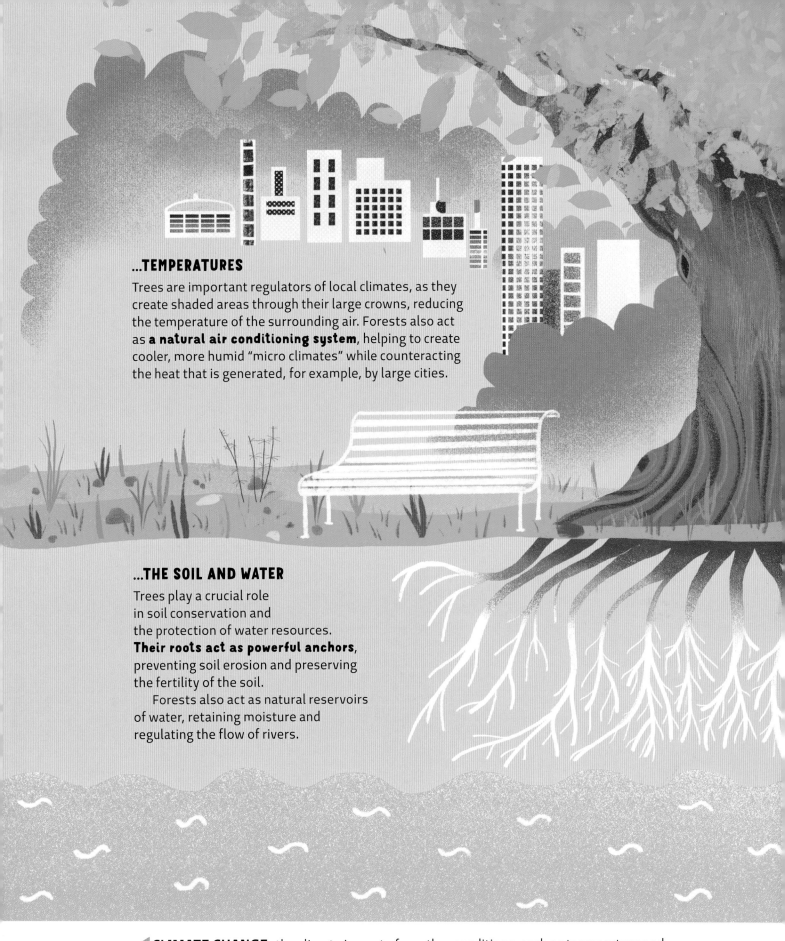

...TEMPERATURES

Trees are important regulators of local climates, as they create shaded areas through their large crowns, reducing the temperature of the surrounding air. Forests also act as **a natural air conditioning system**, helping to create cooler, more humid "micro climates" while counteracting the heat that is generated, for example, by large cities.

...THE SOIL AND WATER

Trees play a crucial role in soil conservation and the protection of water resources. **Their roots act as powerful anchors**, preventing soil erosion and preserving the fertility of the soil.

Forests also act as natural reservoirs of water, retaining moisture and regulating the flow of rivers.

CLIMATE CHANGE: the climate is a set of weather conditions, such as temperature and precipitation, observed over a long period of time; changes to the earth's climate, which in recent decades has been rapid and caused mainly by human activity, is causing a worrisome rise in temperatures seen around the globe.

TREES AND HUMAN EVOLUTION

Over the centuries, wood has been an essential material for humanity!

DOING WITHOUT IT WOULD BE EXTREMELY COMPLICATED! WOOD HARVESTING CAN BE MANAGED SUSTAINABLY BY REPLACING LOGGED TREES AND GIVING FORESTS TIME TO REGENERATE.

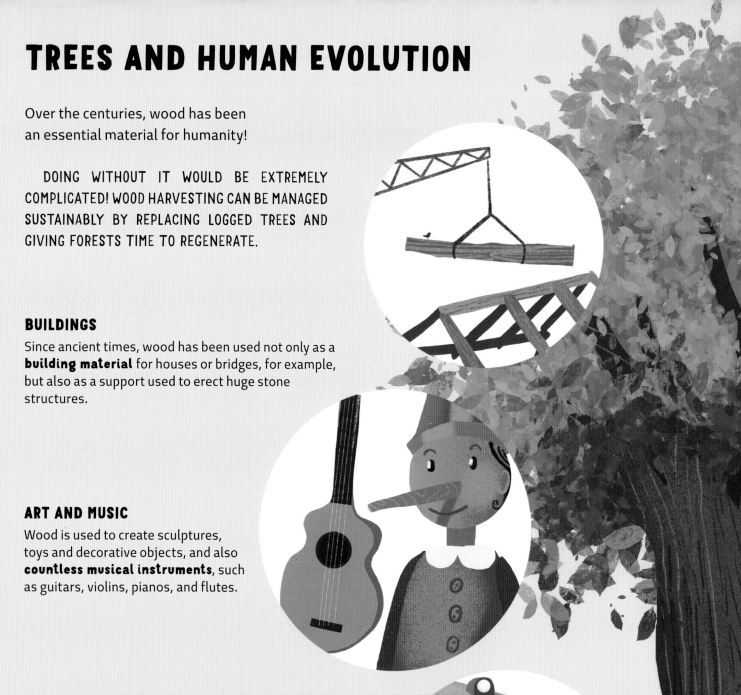

BUILDINGS

Since ancient times, wood has been used not only as a **building material** for houses or bridges, for example, but also as a support used to erect huge stone structures.

ART AND MUSIC

Wood is used to create sculptures, toys and decorative objects, and also **countless musical instruments**, such as guitars, violins, pianos, and flutes.

TRANSPORTATION

The use of wood as a building material for **vehicles such as ships or even trains** has been very common in the past, and even today. For many civilizations, it has even been crucial!

The **Phoenicians**, for example, were able to expand their trade and exploration throughout the Mediterranean Sea **because of the large cedar trees**, whose tall, straight trunks were perfect for building ships.

FUEL

Wood has been used as a **fuel for heating and cooking food for centuries**. Even today, this habit is still widespread in mountainous areas and small towns.

PAPER
One of the most widely used everyday materials is produced from trees. Here's how.

Wood is chopped into very small pieces to make a powder rich in **cellulose**, the main ingredient in paper.

Impurities, such as resin, are removed from the mixture so that the paper is white. At this point, **water** is added, **which** turns the powder into a glue-like paste. This mixture is first spread on a surface that is perfectly flat, then it is pressed to remove the water. It is then dried until it's ready to be cut into sheets of paper.

CAN YOU THINK OF OTHER EVERYDAY USES FOR WOOD?

HEALING TREES AND SACRED TREES

Over the centuries, humankind has learned about the healing properties of various leaves, barks, roots, and resins, capable of offering a wide range of benefits to human health.

TEA TREE

One of the best known medicinal trees is the tea tree, native to Australia.

Its leaves are used to produce an essential oil, known as **tea tree oil**, which is often used to treat skin problems due to its **disinfectant properties**.

NEEM TREE

This tree is native to India. The oil made from its bark and leaves is a disinfectant and also a repellent for some insects. In the area that it comes from, it is used in traditional medicine to **fight parasites**, treat skin diseases, and help **wounds to heal faster**.

GINKGO BILOBA

Native to China, this is a very ancient species of tree. Its leaves contain an ingredient used to **improve blood circulation** and keep our **brains** healthy, preventing age-related disorders such as memory loss.

SINCE ANCIENT TIMES, TREES HAVE BEEN WORSHIPED AND RESPECTED IN MANY CULTURES AND ARE CONSIDERED SYMBOLS OF STRENGTH, WISDOM, AND CONNECTION TO THE SPIRITUAL WORLD.

THE BODHI TREE

The Bodhi Tree is a fig tree considered sacred in **India**, as Buddha is believed to have attained enlightenment while sitting beneath it. Huge specimens can be found in India, carefully cared for by the local population.

OAKS

Oaks were considered sacred among many ancient European cultures, such as the Celts and the Norse. These trees were symbols of **strength**, **wisdom**, **power**, **nobility**, and **longevity**. Because of the meanings attributed to it for centuries, oak trees have been depicted on many noble coats of arms.

THE TREE OF LIFE (BAOBAB)

Widespread in Africa and Madagascar, the baobab is considered to be a sacred tree in many local cultures. It is often called the "**tree of life**" because of its longevity and its importance to the community as a source of food and water for humans and animals.

HOW TO LIVE IN HARMONY

In this book, we've learned a lot about our friends the trees. We understand their **importance to us and our planet**, and we've discovered their strengths and weaknesses.

However, despite our awareness of the gifts offered by trees, we humans sometimes damage entire forest ecosystems.

WHAT CAN EACH OF US, IN OUR OWN SMALL WAY, DO TO HELP THEM?

LET'S RECYCLE!

It is very important to recycle paper, but also to make sure that the paper you buy comes from sustainable forests and to use as much recycled paper as possible!

UNFRIENDLY BEHAVIOR!

Avoid doing things that damage trees, such as carving their bark, tearing off branches or leaves for no reason, and digging near the roots.

BUT THE MOST IMPORTANT THING WE CAN DO IS TO REMIND OURSELVES, WHEN WE ARE IN A FOREST, A PARK, OR ANYWHERE WHERE THERE ARE TREES, THAT WE ARE SURROUNDED BY LIVING BEINGS THAT CAN SENSE WHAT IS AROUND THEM, INCLUDING US!

SO REMEMBER: DON'T TREAT THEM AS THINGS OR AS INANIMATE OBJECTS, BUT AS IMPORTANT PARTS OF THE PLANET THAT WE SHARE WITH THEM.

THE ILLUSTRATORS

ESTER CASTELNUOVO

has a degree in scenography from the Brera Academy of Fine Arts. In addition to her numerous collaborations with publishing houses, Castelnuovo creates animated sets and illustrated backdrops for notable theaters, such as the Piccolo Teatro in Milan, Italy.

VALENTINA FIGUS

has a degree in communication and visual design from the Polytechnic University of Milan. She has worked as a freelancer for several publishing companies, creating interactive digital books, graphic layouts, illustrations, and infographics for educational books.

THE AUTHOR

MASSIMO DOMENICO NOVELLINO

has a personal passion for plants and biodiversity, as well as travel, photography, and writing. With that, he is a PhD candidate at the University of Padua and a teaching assistant at the University of Milan in botany. Novellino has authored several books with the university, including a guide of its botanical garden.

WS whitestar kids™ is a trademark of White Star s.r.l.

© 2024 White Star s.r.l.
Piazzale Luigi Cadorna, 6
20123 Milan, Italy
www.whitestar.it

ISBN 978-88-544-2046-5
1 2 3 4 5 6   28 27 26 25 24

Printed in China
by Dream Color (Hong Kong)
Printing Limited Kowloon, Hk

MIX
Paper from
responsible sources
FSC® C178000
FSC
www.fsc.org